SCIENCE·DISCOVERIES™

GALILEO

AND THE

UNIVERSE

STEVE·PARKER

HarperCollins*Publishers*

Acknowledgments

Photographic credits:
Ancient Art and Architecture Collection: 1, 18 center left
Bridgeman Art Library: 5, 21, 25 top
Mary Evans Picture Library: 3, 8 main picture, 9 top, 12 top and bottom, 13 top right, 20 left
Michael Holford: 8 inset, 11 top right
Magnum/Eric Lessing: 20 right, 23 top
Mansell Collection: 13 bottom, 22
NASA: 27 top
National Portrait Gallery, London: 26
Ann Ronan Picture Library: 7 right, 13 top left, 24 top
Scala: 14 bottom, 18 -19 bottom, 18 top, 19 top
Science Photo Library: 14 top Barney Magrath, 16 NASA, 17 John Sanford, 18 center right NASA, 27 bottom Roger Bessmeyer
Spectrum Colour Library: 10 bottom

Illustrations by Tony Smith
Diagrams by Peter Bull

Galileo and the Universe

Printed in Hong Kong for Imago Publishing.

1 2 3 4 5 6 7 8 9 10

Library of Congress Cataloging-in-Publication Data
Parker, Steve.
    Galileo and the universe / Steve Parker.
        p. cm. — (Science discoveries)
    Includes index.
    Summary: Discusses the life and discoveries of Galileo, the sixteenth- and seventeenth-century mathematician, physicist, and astronomer who challenged ideas more than a thousand years old and changed the course of science.
    ISBN 0-06-020735-3
    1. Galilei, Galileo, 1564–1642—Biography—Juvenile literature.
2. Astronomy—History—Juvenile literature. 3. Astronomers— Italy— Biography—Juvenile literature. [1. Galileo 1564–1642.
2. Scientists.] I. Title. II. Series.
QB36.G2P22 1992
520' .92—dc20
[B]

91-28315
CIP
AC

Contents

Introduction

Science and scientific progress are a vital part of modern life. Inventions such as gasoline engines, computers and nuclear power have changed our way of life dramatically. Scientists continue to ask questions, develop their theories, carry out experiments and make new discoveries. Hardly a week passes without news of an important advance in one or another branch of science.

This was not always so. For centuries, areas of science such as physics were seen as part of a general philosophy of nature. This had been handed down, unquestioned, from thinkers of ancient times, such as Aristotle and Plato. It also fitted neatly with the ideas of the Catholic Church.

Four centuries ago in Italy, Rome was the world center of the Roman Catholic religion (as it is today). The Church was a powerful force in everyday life. Questioning scientific ideas meant challenging the authority of the Church—which could mean a death sentence.

Galileo was an Italian mathematician, physicist and astronomer who succeeded in changing the course of science. He made great advances in many fields of physics. He championed the idea of carrying out experiments to test scientific theories, and of using mathematics to study the results. He was the first to look at the night sky with a telescope, and he made many discoveries about the planets and stars.

By encouraging this break from traditional thinking, Galileo paved the way for the scientific progress that has brought us so much today.

During the life of Galileo, Italy was divided into independent city-states. Each main city and its surrounding area was under the control of a wealthy and powerful family, such as the Medici family in Florence.

St. Peter's in Rome, the heart of the Catholic Church.

Aristotle and the Church

The Greek philosopher Aristotle, who lived from about 384 to 322 B.C., was the main influence on scientific thinking for over 1,800 years.

Aristotle identified two types of motion, called "natural" and "unnatural." In the first type, an object would move up or down. So a stone would naturally fall to the ground, and smoke would rise into the air.

Put simply, "unnatural" motion involved moving horizontally—as when a stone is thrown across a field.

In the Heavens, the movements of the stars were natural, but in a different way from on Earth. Their journeys were circular and never ending, and therefore "perfect" and never changing.

These ideas, although strange and unscientific now, fitted well with the Catholic Church's teachings in Galileo's time. God was the Creator of all things. The heavens, being His Works, were perfect, and could not be changed. But on Earth, things were not perfect. People could cause "unnatural" happenings. The power of the Church made it difficult for free thinkers such as Galileo to challenge Aristotle's teachings.

Chapter One
The Early Years

More than four hundred years ago in Europe, life was very different from today. There were no factories or industries. Most people worked on farms, or in crafts such as pottery and carpentry. Few children went to school, and even fewer could read and write. Books were rare and very expensive, and they were usually written in Latin, the language of scholars and the Church. Science as we learn it today was almost unknown.

Into this world, Galileo Galilei was born on February 15, 1564, in Pisa, northwest Italy. He had two sisters and one brother. His father, Vicenzio Galilei, was a music teacher. The family was not rich, but Galileo soon showed he was a good student and willing to learn, so as a young boy, he had a private teacher. The family moved to Florence in 1574, and he was educated by the monks of the Camaldolese monastery at nearby Vallombrosa.

The swinging lamp

In 1581, while still only 17 years old, Galileo began to study medicine at the University of Pisa. He had vague ideas about becoming a doctor at that time.

It is said that one day in 1581, in Pisa Cathedral, Galileo watched a lamp hung on a long chain from the ceiling. He saw how it swung to and fro in the great, drafty building. He also observed that whether the lamp swung a long way or only slightly, it took the same amount of time for one complete swing back and forth. This observation was not at all what Galileo expected. Later he happened to overhear an interesting geometry lesson at the University.

These events were the beginning of Galileo's interest in the branches of science that we now call physics and mathematics. From 1583, he was taught by a family friend, Ostilio Ricci, who lived in Pisa and was a court tutor for the Duke of Tuscany, the local ruler.

When Galileo was 17 years old, he noticed a chandelier lamp swinging from the ceiling in Pisa Cathedral. He timed the swings, using his pulse as a "clock." Later, he checked his observations with experiments, and made more accurate measurements.

This is what the Italian city of Pisa, in the Tuscany region of Italy, looked like during the late sixteenth century. Previously the center of an independent city-state, with a large fleet of ships, it had been taken over by Florence, in the fifteenth century.

7

Balls, boats and pendulums

In the 1500s, after many centuries of neglect, there was a new interest in the arts—in painting and sculpture, in writing and architecture—and, gradually, in science. This period of new scholarly study is now known as the Renaissance.

Galileo finally left the medical school in Pisa in 1585, partly because his money was running out and partly because he had lost interest in medicine. Over the next few years he was a lecturer at the Academy of Florence. He also experimented with balls, toy boats, pendulums and many other objects. He watched how they fell, floated and swung. He measured and timed their movements and tried to devise mathematical explanations for their motions.

By 1586 Galileo had made use of his studies by inventing a new type of hydrostatic balance. This made him famous across Italy and earned him some money. He also wrote a scientific article about the idea that every object has a "center of gravity," which assists calculations about its movements. This helped him to obtain the appointment of Professor of Mathematics at the University of Pisa in 1589.

This pendulum device meant for keeping time was a design thought up by Galileo the year before his death. It seems that Galileo did not link the swings of a pendulum with timekeeping until late in his career.

These are the arches of the University of Pisa.

Experimental science

The idea of doing experiments was very strange in Galileo's time. For hundreds of years, people had believed the teachings of ancient Greek philosophers, chiefly Aristotle (pictured right), but no one had carried out experiments to check that these ideas were correct. For instance, Aristotle said that heavier objects fall faster than light ones. Galileo carried out many

tests on falling objects. He showed that two different weights of the same size and shape, dropped at the same time, hit the ground together. By such experiments, Galileo helped to establish the modern approach to science, in which ideas are tested to see if they are true.

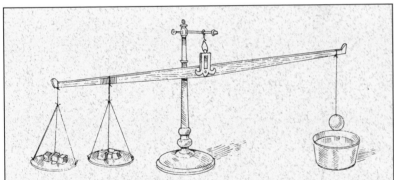

The hydrostatic balance

This device was based on the principle of Archimedes, a famous mathematician who lived eighteen centuries before Galileo. The balance showed that an object immersed in a liquid weighs less than it does in air, by an amount equal to the weight of liquid it displaces, or pushes aside.

The balance could identify the metals from which objects were made. It could also help detect their proportions in alloys, mixtures of metals. This was important because goldsmiths and silversmiths might try to cheat customers by mixing expensive metals with cheap ones.

Chapter Two

The Professor of Mathematics

The Tower experiment

It is said that to prove his new ideas, Galileo climbed to the top of the Leaning Tower of Pisa. Watched by teachers and students, he dropped two balls of the same size but different weights over the edge. The traditional view was that the heavier ball would hit the ground first. But both balls landed together. Even so, the professors would not listen to Galileo's views, which became the center of a great controversy at the University.

Galileo stayed at Pisa for three years. While there, he wrote about moving objects. He studied how they gained speed (accelerated) as they fell or rolled down a slope. He watched how a ball followed a curve when thrown across a courtyard, and he experimented with levers and ramps. He always tried to carry out real-life experiments. He measured and timed what happened, and he calculated the results mathematically.

Many of his observations did not agree with those of Aristotle and other ancient philosophers. Galileo's colleagues at the University became angry. They did not believe that anyone should speak out against the traditional teachings.

The Leaning Tower of Pisa, decorated with white marble, was finished in about 1270. It is 55 meters high, and a cannonball dropped from the lower (north) side would hit the ground in less than three seconds.

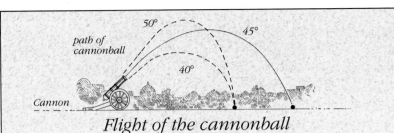

Flight of the cannonball

In his researches on motion, Galileo rolled cannonballs down planks and measured how they fell to the ground. He noted they did not drop straight down off the plank's end, but fell in a curve, and he measured how far lengthwise they traveled from the edge of the plank, and how long they took. The curved path followed by such a cannonball is a parabola.

Galileo found, from tests and mathematical calculations, that to fire a cannonball farthest, the cannon should be fired pointing upward at 45°. He noted that "of other shots, those that exceed or fall short of 45° by equal amounts have equal ranges."

The thermoscope, designed by Galileo while he was a professor at Padua, was used to measure temperature and air pressure.

Professor at Padua

To avoid further conflict, in 1592 Galileo moved to Padua, near Venice, as a professor of mathematics. Here, the authorities allowed people to speak more freely about their work. Galileo was also able to earn more money, but he did not become rich. His father had died in 1591, and Galileo had to take over the family finances. He paid large dowries when his two sisters married, and he gave money to his younger brother, Michelangelo, who was a musician.

Galileo was a professor at Padua for eighteen years. He taught students about geometry and astronomy, and he continued his work on movement and acceleration. He never married, but during his time at Padua, he had two daughters and a son with Marina Camba. During his years in Padua, Galileo invented a mathematical instrument, the proportional compass, which he sold to augment his income. He also studied heat and the effect it has on different liquids. This study led him to develop a simple type of thermometer.

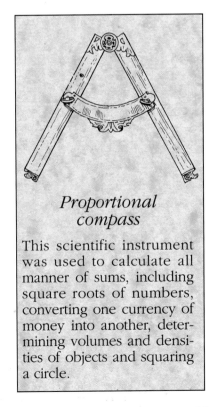

Proportional compass

This scientific instrument was used to calculate all manner of sums, including square roots of numbers, converting one currency of money into another, determining volumes and densities of objects and squaring a circle.

Nicolaus Copernicus (1473–1543) attended the University of Krakow, in present-day Poland, which was famous at the time for mathematics and astronomy. He also traveled to Italy to study at Bologna, Padua and Ferrara. He published his theories of planetary movements in On the Revolutions of the Heavenly Spheres *(1543).*

Johannes Kepler (1571–1630) was a German astronomer who strongly supported the ideas of Copernicus. He is shown here (figure at left) with his patron. Kepler exchanged letters with Galileo, and in 1610 he wrote in praise of Galileo's discoveries with the newly invented telescope.

Copernicus

In about 1597, Galileo read the work of the Polish astronomer Nicolaus Copernicus, who had died more than 50 years earlier. Copernicus had suggested that the Earth and the other planets traveled around the sun. This was quite different from the accepted view of the time, which was that everything circled the Earth. It was widely believed that the Earth was the center of the universe.

Galileo recognized that the ideas of Copernicus fitted his observations about planetary movements, and they also explained his own theories about how the sea's tides rose and fell. Galileo had observed that the rhythm of the tides was linked to the movements of both the moon and the sun.

Kepler

Copernicus' work had been published by another astronomer and mathematician, Johannes Kepler, who was living in Germany. So Galileo wrote privately to Kepler, saying that he thought Copernicus was right. But he was worried about talking openly, because saying that the Earth was not the center of all things would go against the traditional teachings and religious views of the day.

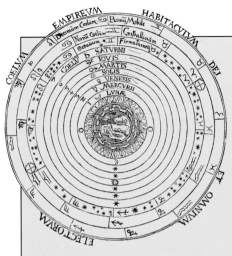

A drawing from 1539 of the solar system, according to the views of ancient scientists such as Aristotle and Ptolemy. The Earth is in the center. Around it are the "spheres" or orbits of the moon and the six planets known at the time, with their Latin names. The sun is between Venus and Mars. The outermost sphere is Habitaculum Dei, *the Abode of God.*

Two views of the solar system

Ptolemy's system—In about the year A.D. 130, the Greek astronomer Ptolemy improved on the work of Aristotle and described how the Earth, moon, sun and other heavenly bodies moved in relation to each other. He believed that the Earth was at the center and stayed still. The other bodies moved around it in combined circular paths. This is known as the geocentric system.

Copernicus' system—In this system, the Earth was not still. It turned, or rotated, once each day. It also moved around the sun, along with all the other planets. So the sun was the center of the solar system. This theory is known as the heliocentric system. Astronomers have since proved it right.

Ptolemy put forward his geocentric view of the universe in his book the Almagest, *about A.D. 130. He worked out the detailed geometric path for each planet as it moved through the heavens, with the Earth at the center. He also produced* Geography, *with maps of the world as it was known at the time. Both books remained popular until the sixteenth century.*

An early French diagram of the Copernican system. The sun is at the center, with the known planets ranged outward. Earth is in its correct position, third from the center, with the moon orbiting it. The moons of Jupiter and Saturn are also shown, orbiting their planets. Galileo saw how much better this system fitted in with his observations.

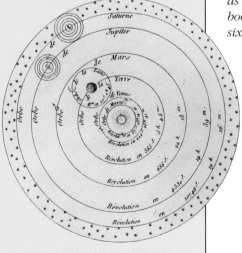

13

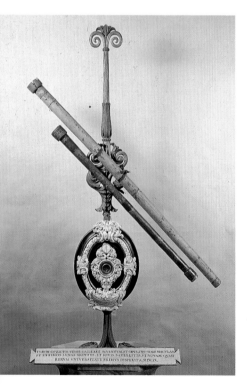

The appearance of three bright comets in 1618 moved Galileo to pursue his study of the heavens. Above is the famous Halley's comet, which, because of its 76-year orbit, became further proof that Galileo's convictions about the universe were right. Below are the telescopes used by Galileo to view the stars.

Chapter Three
Studying the Night Sky

In 1604 the sky was lit by a *stella nova* (meaning new star) far away in the universe. Few people understood what this bright object was. In reality it was an exploding star, a supernova. What it proved to astronomers at the time was that the heavens, as Aristotle and the Church believed, were not "perfect" and unchangeable. It inspired Galileo to further explore his theories about the universe.

In 1607 he published his first book. It was on the proportional compass he had invented (see page 11). Then in 1609 came news from Holland about another invention, which had been devised by Hans Lippershey the previous year. This was the telescope, a new instrument that used lenses to make objects appear much nearer than they were. Galileo began to build his own versions almost at once, and in a few months he had made one that could magnify 32 times. His telescopes were much clearer and more powerful than those of Lippershey. They were the first that could be used to study the night sky in detail, and soon they were being used all over Europe.

Galileo received a rich reward for his work with the telescope. The Venetian governors awarded him a lifetime professorship and increased his pay greatly. His financial worries were over.

Galileo showing his telescope to Church officials. Many of these men were very wary of Galileo's claims.

Parallel light rays from faraway star

Convex lens

Light rays bent (refracted) by lens

Tube housing

focus

eye sees upside-down image

The astronomical telescope

Galileo's telescope used a convex glass lens at one end of the telescope to bend or refract the light rays, so that they are brought together and focused into a clear, sharp, magnified, upside-down image at the other end.

One reason Galileo's early telescopes were so successful was that he worked out a new way to check that the glass lenses were ground and polished to the correct curvature. This gave magnification without too much blurring or distortion.

A revolution in astronomy

In a few short months of stargazing, Galileo made many important discoveries. He published some of these in his book *Starry Messenger* (1610).

He saw that the moon was not smooth, as had been thought, but that it had mountains and craters. He realized that the faint milky band across the sky, the Milky Way, was made of millions of separate stars. He saw that the planet Venus had phases, like the moon, with different parts lit at different times. He also saw moons going around the giant planet Jupiter. He detected dark areas, sunspots, on the sun. And he could just make out that the planet Saturn was not round but elongated. In fact this apparent shape was due to Saturn's rings.

With his telescope Galileo was the first to notice that Saturn did not look round. Later it was discovered that this was because Saturn has rings.

Sunspots

In 1613, Galileo produced *Letters on Sunspots*, about why sunspots move across the disc of the sun. This was his first open support for the Copernican system, suggesting that the sun itself rotated, as well as that the Earth went around the sun. He disagreed that the spots were tiny planets orbiting the Earth, as suggested by the German Christoph Scheiner, a Jesuit observer.

The discovery of moons orbiting Jupiter was especially significant. It showed that the Earth was not at the center of everything, as in Ptolemy's system. Galileo's discoveries caused great argument. Knowing there would be trouble with his colleagues at the University, he decided to move on. He was given the position of court mathematician to the Grand Duke of Tuscany, and he set up home in Florence.

In 1611 Galileo traveled to Rome and showed his telescope to other scientists and important people, including members of the Church. In recognition of his work, he was elected to the Accademia dei Lincei. This was the first scholarly scientific society of the modern age, which had been founded only recently, in 1603.

Then in 1613 Galileo wrote *Letters on Sunspots*, which was published by the Accademia dei Lincei. The book was based on research done using the telescope with which he had won his award to the Accademia. In his book, for the first time, Galileo openly supported the Copernican system. This was to have serious consequences for Galileo.

(top) Galileo was an accurate observer and recorder, as shown by his drawings of the moon's cratered surface in different phases, from his notebooks. Sadly, many of his documents were destroyed because of his troubles with the Church.

(center left) The objective (front) lens from one of Galileo's telescopes was only a few centimeters across. The largest telescope lens today is the refractor at the Yerkes Observatory in Wisconsin. It measures 102 centimeters in diameter.

(center right) A modern photograph of Io, one of Jupiter's moons. Galileo observed that this giant planet had four "stars" (all planets, moons and stars were known by this name at the time). These four are now called the Galilean moons—Io, Europa, Ganymede and Callisto. We have so far discovered a total of sixteen moons in orbit around Jupiter, and a rocky satellite ring.

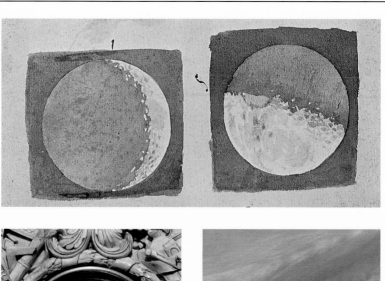

Chapter Four
Trouble with the Church

In Italy in the seventeenth century, the Church was extremely powerful. People who disagreed with its teachings were seen as heretics who should be punished. Galileo knew his views on astronomy would get him into trouble, since the Church believed in the geocentric system. So in 1615 he wrote a letter in his defense, now known as the *Letter to the Grand Duchess Christina*.

In this, Galileo argued for freedom for science. He said that scientists should be able to express their thoughts and opinions, and to carry out experiments to prove or disprove their theories. He warned against people simply believing the traditional teachings of those like Aristotle and Ptolemy, without testing them for themselves and making their own observations and measurements. This plea seems strange today, when experiment is such a central part of science. But it was not so in Galileo's time.

The letter did not succeed. Galileo went to Rome and tried to convince Pope Paul IV of the need for scientific freedom—and that Copernicus was right. But the Pope was not persuaded. In 1616, a church investigation ordered Galileo never to talk or write in support of Copernicus again, under threat of prison.

The Grand Duchess Christina, to whom Galileo wrote in 1615 pleading for freedom of science. The letter was really meant for her son, the Grand Duke of Tuscany.

Florence, capital of the Tuscany region, in Galileo's day. The city was a world center for arts, architecture and finance, especially from the thirteenth to the sixteenth centuries.

Back in Florence, Galileo continued work on physics, motion and mechanics. Some of the results of this work were published in his book *Assayer* (1623). He described how work must begin with the real world, rather than with ancient beliefs. Then in 1623 an old friend of Galileo's, Maffeo Barberini, became the next Pope, Urban VIII. He allowed Galileo to write a balanced book comparing the old and new astronomical theories. This was the *Dialogue Concerning the Two Chief World Systems* (1632).

The triumph of the Dialogue

The *Dialogue Concerning the Two Chief World Systems* is one of the greatest scientific books. It challenged the teachings that there were two sets of natural laws, one for heaven and one for Earth.

Galileo put forward the view that the Earth and human beings were not apart from the heavens. The Earth was a planet, part of the solar system, which was part of an even bigger universe. Humans and all things on Earth were subject to natural laws, which the sciences of physics and mathematics could describe. Whether it was a ball thrown into the air or a planet orbiting the sun, the same laws applied and science could offer an explanation. The book also contained advances in many other areas of physics.

Most books at the time were written in Latin. Galileo wrote the *Dialogue* in Italian, because he wanted everybody to read and understand his work.

The Inquisition

Galileo's *Dialogue* first was approved by the Church authorities. Upon publication, it was greeted as a masterpiece by scientists and philosophers across Europe.

However, it soon became clear that the book was not evenly balanced. Galileo had decided that the scientific evidence supported the Copernican heliocentric system. This meant that much of the accepted scientific knowledge of the time—based on the teachings of Aristotle and the other ancients—must be wrong.

Within a few months, in February 1633, Galileo was back in Rome on trial. The Pope, formerly his friend, was now his enemy. Galileo was accused of breaking his agreement that he would never again support Copernicus and go against the Church and its beliefs. He defended himself strongly in front of the Church Inquisition, saying that scientific observations and facts could not be ignored. But in the end he was forced to admit that he had gone too far. All his books were banned, and copies of the *Dialogue* were ordered burned. Galileo's punishment was prison—for life.

Galileo was prosecuted on "vehement suspicion of heresy," although it is quite possible that some of the documents used as evidence against him, from his previous appearance in 1616, had been "planted." Galileo was made to read out a document admitting he was wrong and saying the Copernican system was false. At the end, however, he is said to have muttered "Eppur si muove"—"Still it moves"—referring to the Earth moving around the sun.

Chapter Five
The Later Years

Galileo was devastated by the sentence of life imprisonment. But the Pope quickly changed this to house arrest. In December 1633 Galileo returned to his home, Villa Arcetri, in the hills near Florence. The house and gardens were his "prison" for the rest of his life.

What do we know of Galileo's personal life? An active and outgoing man, he had many friends, ranging from professors and noblemen to members of the Church, artists and traders. He loved painting and poetry, and he studied literature so that he could write his own works in a clear and entertaining style. This house arrest must have been very frustrating for him. Even during his later years, as his health gradually failed, he was not allowed to leave his villa to visit doctors in Florence.

Galileo was sentenced to life imprisonment on June 21, 1633. However, the Pope reduced this part of the punishment to house arrest, and by December of that year Galileo had returned to his villa near Florence.

Work at Villa Arcetri

Encouraged by his friend the Archbishop of Siena, Galileo soon returned to work at his home. He continued to write, and his great book *Discourses and Mathematical Demonstrations Relating to Two New Sciences Concerning Mechanics* had to be smuggled from Italy because of the ban on his publications. It was printed by Louis Elzevirs at Leiden, Netherlands, in 1638.

Galileo was still a keen astronomer. In 1637 he discovered that the moon had regular librations. These librations are slight "rocking" movements made by the moon, and the result is that we can see more than half of the moon's surface at any one time. The moon rocks because its equator is not at right angles to its axis of spin and because it does not go around the Earth at a regular speed.

Galileo's villa at Arcetri, where he spent the last nine years of his life. Here he wrote the famous book Discourses *and carried on his work in physics, mechanics and mathematics. Many scientists and travelers visited the house, since Galileo was now known throughout Europe, chiefly for his earlier works, the* Starry Messenger *and the* Dialogue.

Two new sciences

Galileo's last main book was *Discourses and Mathematical Demonstrations Relating to Two New Sciences Concerning Mechanics*. It was a summary of his early experiments and his later advances in physics, including his work on motion and the strengths of various substances.

Galileo's own view was that the *Discourses* was the beginning of a new era in the physical sciences. This proved so, since it was one of the main influences on the work of Isaac Newton (see page 27).

The great poet John Milton visited Galileo in 1638, on his travels through France, Switzerland and Italy. Galileo was a keen admirer of literature, especially the Roman poet Virgil and the Italian writer Dante (who had also lived in Florence).

The next year, Galileo became blind. Yet he remained busy and inventive. He wrote letters to many other scientists. Villa Arcetri was visited by famous people such as his long-time friend the Grand Duke of Tuscany, the English poet John Milton, and the English scientist and philosopher Thomas Hobbes. He worked with his pupils Vincenzo Viviani and Evangelista Torricelli, who later became well-known physicists.

The final pardon

Attempts were made to obtain a pardon and free Galileo of his house arrest, but these failed. Galileo himself said that he could not expect a pardon because only the guilty could be pardoned. He was still working on ideas about pendulums, and what happened at the point of impact when two objects collided, when he suffered a fever. He died at Arcetri on January 8, 1642.

Galileo's friends and followers, including the Grand Duke, wanted a fitting burial and tomb for such a great man. But the Church Inquisition in Rome still held the view that Galileo was a condemned heretic. So he was buried in a cemetery and a quiet ceremony was held in the family church, Santa Croce, in Florence. Only in the next century was he given recognition. His remains were moved to a fine tomb in the church of Santa Croce, and Galileo took his rightful place in history as one of the greatest scientists of all time.

Galileo's tomb as it is today, in Florence.

The funeral of Galileo was attended by only family and close friends.

Chapter Six
After Galileo

In Italy, after his death, Galileo's colleagues and their pupils carried on his work. Benedetto Castelli began the science of hydrodynamics, the study of forces and pressures in liquids. Evangelista Torricelli experimented with air pressure and devised an instrument to measure it, the barometer. Bonaventura Cavalieri worked in mathematics and helped to start the branch of science called calculus.

Galileo's discoveries with the telescope had made him famous as the leading astronomer in Europe. Some scientists did not believe his observations, saying that they were caused by the telescope itself, which was a new and unproven invention. However, over the following years others built telescopes, and they showed that Galileo's early sightings were correct. From this firm footing, astronomy developed as a major branch of science.

Apart from astronomy, Galileo was best known in Europe for his two main books, *Dialogue* and *Discourses*. Because of the Church ban, his writings were forbidden in Italy, although secret copies were available. They were also smuggled to other countries, where they were published. Scientists read them eagerly and developed the ideas further.

Isaac Newton (1642–1727) was born in the year of Galileo's death. He took up the advances that Galileo had made and, in a more receptive society, was able to bring about great changes in the study of science.

Telescopes and astronomy have changed enormously since Galileo's time. Most big modern telescopes are reflectors, using central mirrors, rather than lenses as in Galileo's refractors. The Shane telescope, at the Lick Observatory on Mount Hamilton, California, has a main mirror 3 meters across (below). The Space Shuttle, itself an amazing feat of mechanical and electronic engineering (left), launches special telescopes into space. Since these do not have to look through the atmosphere, they can see farther and more clearly into the universe than any telescope on the planet's surface.

Galileo hoped that his last book, the *Discourses*, would begin a new era in scientific freedom and investigation. It dealt with various areas of physics such as heat, light and sound. It covered acceleration, falling objects and other aspects of motion and mechanics. It showed how new theories should be tested by experiments, and how mathematics could analyze the results. It even touched on the idea of "infinitesimals," substances divided into their smallest possible parts. We know of these today as atoms and elementary particles.

The year Galileo died, another great scientist, Isaac Newton, was born in England. Within thirty years Newton was building on the work of Galileo, the French mathematician and philosopher René Descartes, the English chemist Robert Boyle and other scientists. In 1687 he published his monumental book, usually called *Principia*, which many experts agree is the greatest scientific work of all time. Helped largely by Galileo, the modern age of science had begun.

The World in Galileo's Time

	1550 - 1575	1576 - 1600
Science	**1551** Konrad von Gesner writes *Historia Animalium*, the first work on animals since the ancients **1564** Galileo is born **1569** Gerard Mercator founds the science of cartography, or mapmaking	**1589** Galileo becomes professor of mathematics at Pisa **1590** Zacharias Janssen invents the first microscope
European Expansion	**1559** Tobacco is brought to Europe from North America **1571** Spain conquers the Philippines	**1584** Potatoes are first imported into Europe from South America **1585** John Davis tries to find a northern sea route between Europe and Asia; he fails but finds a strait near Greenland, later named Davis Strait
Politics	**1562** Civil wars of religion, between Catholics and Huguenots, begin in France **1569** Pope names Cosimo de' Medici Grand Duke of Tuscany **1571** Ottoman Empire is defeated by Spain in the Battle of Lepanto	**1581** Russia begins its conquest of Siberia **1588** The English fleet, commanded by Francis Drake, defeats the Spanish Armada **1600** Oyo Empire at its height in what is now Nigeria and Benin
Arts	**1560s** Mogul school of miniature painting flourishes in India **1569** Peter Breughel the Elder dies **1570** Palladio writes his *Treatise on Architecture*	**1596** Italian artist Michelangelo da Caravaggio completes The Supper at Emmaus **1600** First performance of William Shakespeare's *Hamlet*

1601 Danish astronomer Tycho Brahe dies

1604 The supernova awakens Galileo's interests in astronomy; the explosion is also recorded by Johannes Kepler, and by astronomers in China and Korea

1638 Galileo's last great book, the *Discourses*, summarizes his work in physics

1641 Galileo invents the first pendulum clock

1642 Galileo dies
Isaac Newton is born

1608 Jamestown, Virginia, becomes the first permanent English settlement in North America

1610 France establishes the colony of Quebec in North America

1640 Sugarcane introduced by Europeans into Brazil and the West Indies

1642 Tasman explores Tasmania and New Zealand

1646 England occupies the Bahamas

1605 Akbar, third Mogul Emperor of India and one of its greatest rulers, dies

1618 Thirty Years' War starts in Germany and soon spreads to central Europe

1621 Native Americans and Pilgrims join together in Thanksgiving feast

1642 English Civil War begins

1644 Ming Dynasty is overthrown in China

1630 Treaty of Madrid ends war between England and Spain

1602 Kabuki theatre begins in Japan

1604 English poet Christopher Marlowe publishes *Doctor Faustus*

1607 *La Favola d'Orfeo* by Claudio Monteverdi, the first true opera

1632 Rembrandt paints *The Anatomy Lesson*

1636 Harvard College is founded in Massachusetts as the first American university

1639 The first printing press is established in North America

29

Glossary

air pressure: the weight of the air in the atmosphere around the Earth, pressing on objects. Air pressure is just over 1 kilogram per square centimeter at sea level. It decreases with altitude—up a mountain or in a plane—and is zero in space.

astronomy: a branch of science relating to the study of the stars and planets and all natural phenomena beyond Earth.

axis: a real or imaginary line around which something rotates. On Earth the axis passes through the North and South poles.

calculus: a branch of mathematics that deals with changing quantities over time. Many branches of science, such as physics, use calculus to develop theories and solve problems.

Catholic: having to do with the Roman Catholic Church, which is the largest group within the Christian religion and is headed by the Pope in Rome.

center of gravity: a point inside or outside an object; if the object can be supported at this point, it will be perfectly balanced. In a ball, the center of gravity is exactly in the center.

convex: curving or bulging outward. A convex lens has two outward-curving surfaces, so it is fatter in the middle than around the edges; opposite of concave.

equator: an imaginary line around the Earth at its widest point, midway between the North Pole and South Pole.

geocentric: having the Earth at the center. Geocentric theory says the planets, moon, sun, stars and other heavenly bodies move around the Earth, which is at the center and stays still. See also heliocentric.

geometry: a branch of mathematics that deals with lines, flat shapes such as circles and squares, and solid shapes such as spheres and cubes. It uses mathematical equations to find length, area and volume.

heliocentric: having the sun at the center. In the heliocentric, or Copernican, theory, the planets (including Earth) and their moons move around the sun, which is at the center. See also geocentric.

heretics: people who go against the accepted beliefs and teachings of a religion, and especially those of the Catholic Church.

hydrodynamics: a branch of physics that studies the pressures, forces and movements in fluids. Also called hydraulics.

Inquisition: an agency of the Roman Catholic Church that searched out heretics.

Latin: the language of ancient Rome and the Roman Empire. In medieval times it was used in important speeches and writings by the Church, scholars and educated people, but is rarely used today.

lenses: pieces of transparent material such as glass, specially shaped to alter the direction of light rays. See also convex.

levers: rods, bars or similar long, rigid objects that pivot at one point, the fulcrum, and which can be used for moving heavy weights. A crowbar and a see-saw are types of levers.

mathematics: a branch of science that deals with quantities and the relationship between numbers

orbits: the paths traced by moons as they go around planets, or by planets as they go around stars. The orbits of the Earth and other planets around the sun are not circles but oval shaped, or elliptical.

parabola: a bowl-shaped line whose ends curve less and less, looking as if they will become parallel (unlike the line of a circle, whose curve is constant). A stone thrown across a field follows a parabola.

philosophy: the study of human knowledge, beliefs and thoughts. It affects many aspects of our lives, such as how we know things, why we believe in right and wrong, and how we define values.

physics: a branch of science that deals with the properties of matter and energy.

proportional compass: an early type of calculating device, with two arms linked by a pivoted joint. The answer to a calculation was found by moving the arms to a certain position and reading where the different rows of numbers crossed.

reflectors: objects, such as mirrors, that reflect light, sound or heat.

square root: a number which, when multiplied by itself, will produce a given number. Since 3 times 3 equals 9, 3 is the square root of 9.

squaring a circle: finding a square equal in area to a given circle.

Sunspots: dark areas that move across the surface of the sun, usually lasting for a few weeks. They are the result of disturbances in the sun's incredibly powerful magnetic field. They are 20,000 kilometers or more across.

supernova: an exploding star, which suddenly becomes much brighter over hours or days and can be seen even in daylight. It then slowly fades away over days and weeks. Only three supernovas have been recorded in our part of the universe — in 1054, 1572, and 1604 (the one Galileo saw).